Essa

Lauren Lownes

BookLeaf
Publishing

Presentation by *BookLeaf Publishing*

Web: www.bookleafpub.com

E-mail: info@bookleafpub.com

ISBN: 9789357697088

First edition 2023

DEDICATION

To everyone I've met over the last few months who
has inspired me to be something more that I am.

This is the first step.

At the Study Room Table

I sipped my coffee, etching verbs and nouns.
You watched your phone, breathing poison laws.
The halls and stairways: always leading down
To rows and rows of open-locked doors.
I read and read, and never anything thought.
You spoke and spoke, and never anything said.
At the study room table, within these painted walls,
Our puppeteered bodies: suspended, dead.
I longed at skyscraper shadows and realised
The windows were barred in this prison torture fort.
And so you held my head in your hands as I cried
For the future that I had already lost and for the past
      that never ended and for the present that scraped my
      bones against the ground like a chalkboard.
And then I sipped my coffee, here, again.
And then you watched your phone, here, again.

The Instructions

Go to school and work hard, harder.
(Help) no-one, and don't expect (help).
(Failure) is because (of) your own incompetence,
Not because of (the system we built).

Go to university, (if you can) get in,
If you can't, drink your life away.
(Learn to think) like everyone else.
You'll be happy if you never (question) anything.

Work. It doesn't matter where.
(The) only (purpose) of anything is to pass the time.
Fifty years, if (you're lucky).
Marry and have kids. Tell yourself (this is enough).

Travel, (if you can. Read), not too much.
We would prefer you just sit in front of your TV
And absorb (everything) we tell you,
(Or) fill your mind with emptiness. Whatever.

Then (die).

Red

Like fresh bruises, red,
Like a cross on a page
next to a name.

Like flying ribbons, red,
Like the glamour of death
In a rugby game.

Now people won't
kill themselves
(angels of Flanders)
because it could
save anyone, but
because it could
look good, or
sound good, or
be made into
a statue…

Or left some roses, red,
Or a tag on a Celebrity's
Story, some fame.

So wear your poppy, red,
and sing:
Dulce et decorum est pro nothing mori.

The End

I hunch my shoulders,
Click my pen.
The end. The end.
The end.

Please let me hide
And play pretend.
The end. The end.
The end.

The sun may come
To rise but then,
Again, again,
Again,

The dark will fight
To make amends.
The end. The end.
The end.

The Waiting Room

Rest your head on my shoulder, please.
We've been here for hours in the bleach white cube
And I'm worried you haven't slept or dreamed
Of what might await when we leave this room.

I see a valley with trickling waterfalls,
And songbirds dancing to their own songs,
And us, barefoot on the muddy floor.
I am trying the see this, beyond the old rusted lock.

Tell me what you see behind the muted white.
Not the woman unconscious in the corner, no,
Nor the man with blood trickling down his neck,
You have to look further, deeper: dream.

We'll drive ourselves insane in this bleach white cube,
Waiting and waiting and waiting. But wait:
If we can convince ourselves none of it's true
There's a chance we might make it, unscathed, to the gate.

Falling

Yet: as we stand here on this rocky cliff
You could hold my hand.
You could hold my hand and I would be able to stop you
From falling.

Or if my starved limbs were too fragile,
And would crumble under the weight of another life,
I would hold your hand,
Tighter,
And fall with you into the endless night.

The World Between Us

You're warm, like a blanket around me at night.
The cold metal of my laptop.
I feel like I'm lying in summer's sunlight.

You're quiet, like piano ballads in a café.
The alarm in the black morning.
I don't jump. I'm not frightened from slumber awake.

Your smile, it lights up the room with a glow.
The LED light bright on my desk.
I see better with a light that's soft and low.

'The Bell Jar'

If someone ever asked me,
"What's the best bit of 'The Bell Jar' by Sylvia Plath?"
I would be too embarrassed to admit
I had never read it.

You once told me,
While we were giggling over her suicide,
That you only liked the description of food at the
    beginning.
I would probably tell them that.

That scares me sometimes.

In your Billie Eilish style Carhartt jacket,
In my room filled with cute things from you,
In your voice I can hear even when you're not there,
In my words that echo unintentionally yours,
You bled into me.

And I don't know where I am anymore.

But then,
I look over at you,
And your black painted fingernails are typing up the titles
    of French films.
And I think: maybe this is supposed to happen.
Maybe this is okay.

Talking

Listen to me.
I'm a water bottle with
a low centre of gravity.

Falling, falling,
A coin landing on its
side. The moment, the hesitation

Before I speak,
Before I say something
I might regret, I might not mean

What I'm saying.
What am I saying?
Please listen to me.

I'm trying, I'm trying.
My heart doesn't speak
English or poetry.

But please understand.

Unsent Messages

I hope you know
that when I took you to see my dog
curled up on her chair like she hadn't a care
in the world
but warmth and comfort and treats and toys:

that meant that I love you.

ERROR: UNSENT
04/02/2022 11:11PM

A Lonely Writer

I sit

                            alone

      with pen and paper.

Snap. Wilde.

      Woolf and her swimming dancers.

            Brontë's haunting hunting moors.

                  Churchill's voices battling. More.

                        Feverish.

                      Scribbling desperate

Vessels of literary divinity.

I'm

                    numb

      and empty.

A blank page makes me feel nauseous.

Outer space

white knuckles, pain-carved
face screaming, grasping
nothing. nothing. nothing.

i can't reach you

i can't save you

i swim to death in outer space.

To the Dead Woman

She left me her last painting,
The one she knew would be her last,
Before she became nothing,
Silent, a spec of dust or ash.

It's the bench by the duck pond
Where she used to walk her dog.
Warm watercolours filled with fond
Memories, slightly misty with fog.

Like her glasses when she drank her tea,
Like my eyes on the Black Day,
When I sat on this bench to see
Why she loved it before, forever, she went away.

But I realise now death is not forever,
Like this pond where we never sat together.
You are not gone, though the sand in the hourglass falls,
In fact, you are here, hanging on my wall.

The Room

Four walls are papered. Muted florals lurk
Behind a bookshelf on the left. It's filled
With Austen, Shelley, French philosophers –
The elegant words that fill my thoughts, that build
My actor's script. On the right: a record player
That's stuck on the same three notes, again,
And again, and again, and again, like a prayer
Or devil's chant. I don't know how to make
It stop. The mirror wall is blinding, each
So small and bent I only see fractions,
Moments of myself, too far to reach.
Above the desk on the final wall, hanging
Is my portrait, like a traitor or a Queen.
And all I do is buzz against the window and dream.

Betting

She's just walked into the coffee shop
With a grey Bram Stoker tote bag.
I bet she's never actually read him,
She just wants people to think she has.

I bet she'll get an oat milk latte.
"Hi, can I get a double espresso?"
Espresso. Of course. You're just too dark
For a drink weakened with milk, aren't you?

She sits at the table next to me,
And opens her stickered laptop.
I bet all she's thinking is "Does the guy
At the table next to me think that I'm hot?"

"Or that I'm as cool as I'm trying to be?"
I bet this is why she came, to be seen
In all her faux mysterious glamour.
I bet when she leaves, all she'll think about's me.

Small

Though I began as a Doll's Minuet, I learned to tower
over the men and the Gods. But my Amazonian
canopies frightened their brittle hedgerows
and so they took an axe to my knees
and I crippled under the weight of
their fuelled eyes and the weight
of my worth until every mirror
was stretched and bent like
my vision and this world
which scrunched me
up like a bit of
scrap paper
smaller
small
…

Let me take up the space I deserve.

Villain Elle

Bound up in dollhouse daydreams, waters taken
By frills and seams and zips sewn in:
The might of vast and tidal seas - misshapen.

Red-ribboned museums – uncut, unshaken –
Tied me shut. The flowers black, and so thin,
Bound me in dollhouse daydreams. I'm taken:

The Ballerina Princess Doll forsaken.
Tried, struggled, donned the chainmail.
The chains of vast and tidal seas are broken.

They heave, hungry, desperate in depths unimagined.
Silk slits in wrists.
Gagged unconscious over kitchen sinks. They'll awaken

And overflow in roared defiance, howling hurt:
I am more, I am more, I am more
Than a lost and scared and searching child:

I am the forest and the moon and the ocean.
I am the terrifying guardian, the master mistress.
I unbind myself and this world so she can breathe
As the tidal seas under my ghostly light.

Alone

I wonder if I can touch the ceiling.

                    all the way.

        if I can reach

I wonder

I wonder if it's worth trying.

    I left my straighteners on.

    Whoops. Off, off.

Lights off too.

I like to dance in the dark. I feel free

here. Spinning and twirling I'm Odette

I'm Alice I'm alone!

Alone!

alone.

I'm happy now but what if I stayed alone forever.

Lights back on, I think.

I knocked a book off my shelf.

    Waiting for Godot.

    Hmm.

    Never mind.

I wonder if I can touch the ceiling.

The Answer

whisper it softly
in my ear
I promise I'll never tell
a soul
in this silent place
where winter whistles
under my skin.

give me something,
please,

the answer.

Ingram Content Group UK Ltd.
Milton Keynes UK
UKHW020635120623
423291UK00014B/584